Reviewers are applauding

"How to be Your Own Best Friend!"

"A kind of psychiatric pep talk . . . directed at people who hate or despise themselves . . . *people who have the patience to learn to operate a car but won't be bothered learning how to operate themselves.*"

—*New York Times*

"What (the Berkowitzes) unearthed . . . is a too-often-forgotten form of human intercourse called getting to know *me*."

—*Chicago Tribune Syndicate*

"This compassionate book is a wonderful prescription for The Blahs . . . an antidote to weariness, discouragement or loneliness."

—*Los Angeles Times*

"In essence, the authors say stop messing up your adult life with inappropriate emotional responses carried over from childhood, and stop putting yourself down. Then they tell you how."

—*Detroit Free Press*

"If there were a magic potion for living that could be bottled and sold over the counter, you can be sure it would be a best seller. But because there is none, Mildred Newman and Bernard Berkowitz have devised a formula to help people live more meaningful lives and give them courage in overcoming the hang-ups that keep them from being happy."

—*Oakland Tribune*

"Read it over and over. It's truly enjoyable, leaving the reader with a sense of relief, knowing there is logical reason for anxiety and frustration."
—*Hartford Courant*

"Seductively jargon free, presented in neat question-and-answer format. Supergull may have competition at the cash register."
—*Houston Chronicle*

"How to achieve emotional well-being . . . in clear, nontechnical language . . . good, informative reading for anyone interested in the sources of mental ease and dis-ease."
—*Library Journal*

"A lot of Beautiful People seem to have grooved on *How To Be Your Own Best Friend*. Their ecstatic testimonials glow about how this little book has changed their lives. Maybe it will change yours too . . ."
—*Minneapolis Tribune*

"It's important to listen to ourselves and if we become our own best friends we can be happy. This is an excellent book of advice."
—*Pensacola News*

"Discover sensible advice on how to give up childhood, accept yourself and your own maturity and deal with life on your own two feet."
—*Dallas Times Herald*

"Packs a wow of wallop . . . everybody's talking about it."
—*Boston Herald American*

A Conversation
with Two Psychoanalysts

How to Be Your Own Best Friend

Mildred Newman &

Bernard Berkowitz

with Jean Owen

BALLANTINE BOOKS • NEW YORK

Library of Congress Catalog Card Number: 73-4029

SBN 345-24333-1-150

This edition published by arrangement with
Random House, Inc.

First Open Market Edition: April, 1974
First U.S. Edition: October, 1974

Printed in the United States of America

BALLANTINE BOOKS
A Division of Random House, Inc.
201 East 50th Street, New York, N.Y. 10022
Simultaneously published by
Ballantine Books, Ltd., Toronto Canada

To those who have helped us become our own best friends—each other, parents, children, patients, teachers, friends, and colleagues

How to
Be
Your Own
Best
Friend

Introduction

When Thoreau remarked that most men live lives of quiet desperation, he could not have foreseen how noisy that desperation would become. Modern man may suffer, like his forebears, but he does not suffer in silence. Our malaise is articulate; we talk about our troubles. More escape hatches may be open to us today, and we eagerly jump the chute. Work has always been available; we can now take further refuge in infinite varieties of entertainment or let a 747 remove us from the scenes of our discontent. But more and more, what's bothering us is up for discussion.

We talk, of course, about what's wrong with the world, about war and welfare, prices and pollution. But we also talk more frankly than ever before about what's awry in our inner world, about frustration and boredom and anxiety, about difficulties with marriage and sex, about the lack of fulfillment in our lives. We may not be any unhappier than our ancestors, but one thing is clear: we do not accept misery as our natural state. Resignation is not for us; if we are unhappy, we feel cheated, displaced, left out, like someone who missed the golden ring. And we protest, either individually or collectively—as in the cry of women's liberationists—our right to meaningful work and satisfying lives. We take very seriously the pursuit of happiness and believe we deserve better than we've got.

Or do we? We state our grievances and readily locate their causes: our jobs, our husbands, our unhappy childhoods. And many of us take steps to remove the offenders: we change careers, divorce, and go to psychoanalysts. Yet the rising decibels of our complaint make one wonder. Are we really doing all we can to make our lives more rewarding?

Granting that we live in a time of social upheaval and dissolving values, where man's chances of survival are anybody's guess, we also have open to us more options than any previous generation. To put it mildly, we don't seem to be making the most of them. Why don't we, and how can we? These questions were posed to two Manhattan psychoanalysts, Dr. Bernard Berkowitz and Mildred Newman, a husband and wife who separately and together (working with groups) are engaged in helping people do better with their lives. Our probing conversation follows.*

---

*For the purpose of coherence, the responses are a composite, as if only one psychoanalyst is speaking.

The Conversation

People say they want to be happy; yet real happiness seems like the impossible dream. Everyone reaches for it so desperately, but for many of us it never seems to come any closer. What are we doing wrong? Why are so many people dissatisfied in so many ways? Is it the times we live in? Do we expect too much? Do we want the wrong things?

Well, it's not as bad as all that. There are plenty of people who are having a wonderful time with their lives; they are living to the

hilt and love every minute of it. But they don't talk about it much; they are busy doing it. They don't usually write articles or go to analysts. Yet it's true; not enough people have that sense of zest in their daily lives. Too many people have just not mastered the art of being happy.

You call it an art. Do you think it is something that can be learned, like dancing or making pottery? But I should think you're either happy or you're not. You can't decide to be happy. You can do a lot of things, but I don't see how you can make happiness. You can go after the things you hope will make you happy, but you really don't know until after you get them whether they will.

In a sense that's true. But the way you put it is part of the problem that many people have in their pursuit of happiness. They think there is something that will make them happy if they can just get hold of it. They expect happiness to happen to them. They don't see it's something they have to *do*. People will go to a lot of trouble to learn French or physics or scuba diving. They have the patience to learn to operate a car but they won't be bothered learning how to operate themselves.

That's a funny idea. You make it sound as if we should be standing at our own controls and pushing buttons. Shouldn't the art of living be more natural than that?

Maybe it should, but for most of us it's not. We are not born with the secret of how to live, and too many of us never learn it.

There is nothing cold-blooded or mechanical about it, but there are many things we have to learn to do.

For example?

The first thing is to realize that we've probably been looking in the wrong place. The source is not outside us; it is within. Most of us haven't begun to tap our own potential; we're operating way below capacity. And we'll continue to as long as we are looking for someone to give us the key to the kingdom. We must realize that the kingdom is in us; we already have the key. It's as if we're waiting for permission to start living fully. But the only person who can give us that permission is ourselves. We are accountable only to ourselves for what happens to us in our lives.

We must realize that we have a choice: we are responsible for our own good time.

It still seems like a strange idea. If it is up to us, if we can push a magic switch and turn on happiness, why doesn't everyone just do it?

There is no magic switch. But there is an attitude. To take responsibility for our lives means making a profound change in the way we approach everything. We do everything we can to avoid this change, this responsibility. We would much rather blame someone or something for making us feel unhappy than take the steps to make us feel better. We even talk about our own feelings as if they were visitors from outer space. We say, "This feeling came over me," as if we were helpless

creatures overwhelmed by mysterious forces, instead of simply saying, "I felt that way." We speak as if our feelings change from sunny to stormy like the weather, over which we have no control. This meteorological view of our emotions is very useful; it takes us off the hook for the way we feel. We diminish ourselves, just in order to push away the chance of choice.

You know, I really find that hard to accept. I mean, feelings are mysterious; they come and go, and most of the time you don't know why. If I am angry or upset about something, I can stop myself from breaking dishes or maybe from breaking into tears, but I can't just stop being upset or miserable. I'm not sure I would even want to. After all, if something has happened to hurt me, then I have a right to feel that hurt.

You certainly do. You have a right to your feelings, your painful feelings just as much as your happier ones. To feel all that you can feel is to be truly human. But too often people cling to unpleasant feelings; they even court them. Without fully realizing what they are doing, they actually bring them about. They do things that make them feel bad and then they say, "I couldn't help myself." What most people mean when they say that is "I didn't help myself." But we can all help ourselves.

Can we really? That's an exciting and lovely thought. I would like to hold on to that. How can we do it?

In so many ways. First, you have to make a very basic decision: do you want to lift yourself up or put yourself down? Are you for yourself or against yourself? That may seem

like a strange question, but many people are literally their own worst enemy. If you decide you want to help yourself, you can choose to do the things that make you feel good about yourself instead of the things that make you feel terrible. Why should you do what gives you pain when it is just as easy to give yourself joy? That's an important question to ask yourself.

People worry about pollution. But the harm we do to ourselves is a lot more dangerous than the damage we do to the environment. We don't need television or comic strips to pollute our minds; we do a much more efficient job of it ourselves. Nobody has to be told how to put himself down; when people are looking for faults or shortcomings, they have no trouble finding them or inventing them if they don't really exist. For many people, finding the things that help them feel good about themselves is a real challenge. It's as if they had blinders on that shut out all the bright spots.

But there are plenty of people who see nothing but their bright spots; they think they're quite satisfactory as they are, and if anything is wrong, it is with somebody else, not them.

Of course. But they don't really believe it. Those who are working that hard to convince themselves—and others—how great they are, are also shutting something out. They can't see their faults because they're afraid they've got nothing else. They think their choice is between being perfect and being the worst thing that ever lived. The trouble is, it's very hard to give up that way of looking at yourself, because it is based on refusing to look into yourself. And to change, you really must look into yourself to see what you're doing wrong. You must be able to see the ways you're pulling yourself down and decide that isn't what you want to do. Then you can start doing the things that give you pride and pleasure in living.

Such as?

Such as being aware of your own achievements. When you do something you are
proud of, dwell on it a little, praise yourself
for it, relish the experience, take it in. We're
not used to doing that, for ourselves or for
others. When things go wrong, they call attention to themselves. When things run well,
we must actively bring them to our attention.

It is up to us to give ourselves recognition.
If we wait for it to come from others, we feel
resentful when it doesn't, and when it does,
we may well reject it. It is not what others
say to us that counts. We all love praise, but
have you ever noticed how quickly the glow
from a compliment wears off? When we compliment ourselves, the glow stays with us. It
is still good to hear it from others, but it
doesn't matter so much if we have already
heard it from ourselves. This is the tragedy
of some marvelous performers, who need end-
less applause to tell them how great they are,
but who feel a chill as soon as they enter their

dressing rooms. They have never heard it from themselves.

I suppose it's like the people who have to prove something over and over again, because they never really believe it, or buy things over and over because of something they feel, inside, they don't really possess— the people who can never get enough of anything.

Yes, they're still looking in the wrong place. It's supposed to be what Don Juan was doing in all those beds. We can see the craziness of it clearly when we look at such extreme examples. But we all fail to appreciate ourselves enough. If someone is on a diet for a week and goes off it for a day, the overeating is nothing compared with the orgy of self-

recrimination ne then indulges in. What about the week he was on the diet? He should give himself credit for that and go right back on it, if that is what he wants for himself. The pitfall is this: very likely it was not so much the food he couldn't resist on the eighth day as the temptation to tear down the wonderful self-image he was building all week long. That's something many of us find hard to take: really feeling good about ourselves. When we "hate ourselves the morning after," we should ask where we get our biggest kick —from our activities the night before or from wallowing in self-reproach the following day.

But what if you do feel lousy about yourself? That's a real feeling, too, isn't it? How can you tell someone to do things to make him feel good if he really does think he's a terrible person?

I suppose if someone said, "Look, I'm a terrible person and I like it that way; leave me alone," there isn't much I could tell him. But chances are he wouldn't mean it. Most people are quite unhappy about making themselves miserable; there is usually a severe inner struggle going on. Part of the person is pushing himself down, but another part is crying out that that's not where he belongs. It's a question of having some compassion for yourself. So when you do something that makes you feel bad inside, ask yourself whether that's the way you want to feel. If not, stop doing what makes you feel that way. Instead, do the things that make you feel good about yourself.

Since you seem to know so many secrets, what are some of the other things that people can do?

They really aren't secrets. People know so much more than they're willing to admit. They're keeping secrets from themselves. Some of them are so simple. One fundamental thing, for example, is to meet your own expectations. If you have housework or homework or some other work to do, and you are tempted to let it slide, ask yourself how you will feel if you put it off. If you sense that you will be a little disgusted with yourself, then go ahead and do the job, and let yourself savor the feeling you get from having done it. Enjoy the experience of being in charge of yourself. It's quite exhilarating. Housework and homework may be a small part of life, but how you feel about yourself throughout the day is life itself. And this process of imagining how you will feel about doing something can turn up some surprises, too. You may discover that doing something other than housework will make you feel even better about yourself that particular day. You may decide to write a poem instead.

Isn't that encouraging people to be awfully self-centered? I have this vision of a woman greeting her husband with a possessed gleam in her eye when he comes home at night. He looks around in dismay at crying babies and unmade beds and asks, "Where's dinner?" and she waves a piece of paper at him and says, "I wrote a poem instead!"

I think very few women would genuinely feel better about themselves if they wrote a poem at that price—at least not more than once. People rarely feel good about themselves for being unkind to others. If something like that happened, I suspect the woman would feel elated but also distressed. And if her poetic urge continued, she would have to make some other choices. Could she manage to write poetry and take care of her family, too? If not, how important was the poetry to her? If it turned out to be something she very much needed to do, she would have to try to get help with her other responsibilities. Maybe her husband would be willing to do more. And, of course, some artists find

that marriage and a family just aren't for them, and they choose their art. That's all right, too. I think one of Katherine Anne Porter's husbands said to her about the failure of their marriage, "But you were already married." We must establish our priorities.

You know, a lot of women's liberationists argue that day care should be widely available so that mothers aren't forced to stay home with their children and stagnate. I'm not against day care or careers for women. But having children is—or ought to be—a choice. If women want to have babies, they should. If they don't want to raise children, they shouldn't have them. But once they do, they have a certain responsibility. If they want to try to have both a family and a career, that's their decision. They are taking on a tough challenge, and it's up to them to meet it. They can lobby for day-care centers if they like, but they shouldn't feel like victims.

But what if you can't manage everything you'd like to do—few of us can—and you have to make choices? When does doing good things for yourself become pure self-indulgence?

Doing what makes you feel good about yourself is really the opposite of self-indulgence. It doesn't mean gratifying an isolated part of you; it means satisfying your whole self, and this includes the feelings and ties and responsibilities you have to others, too. Self-indulgence means satisfying the smallest part of you, and that only temporarily.

It does mean being self-centered enough to care for yourself and to take care of yourself. If you don't learn how to do that, you can never care properly for others. The Bible says, "Love thy neighbor *as* thyself," not "better than" or "instead of" thyself. If we cannot love ourselves, where will we draw our love for anyone else? People who do not love themselves can adore others, because adoration is making someone else big and

ourselves small. They can desire others, because desire comes out of a sense of inner incompleteness, which demands to be filled. But they cannot love others, because love is an affirmation of the living, growing being in all of us. If you don't have it, you can't give it.

Charity begins at home.

Yes. You can see the difference between love and what looks like love, very clearly, in relations between parents and children. Parents always claim that they are acting out of love for their children, but it's easy to see when they're not. When a parent "sacrifices" for a child, you know there's something wrong because of the way the child reacts.

The child feels guilty, not grateful, because what he's getting is not out of love but out of self-denial. No one really wants the fruits of someone else's self-denial. Self-denial is one of the worst kinds of self-indulgence. It is feeding the part of you that feels worthless. No one benefits from that. This doesn't mean you can't sometimes decide to give things up. But that is a choice you make, and it is done out of self-regard, not self-hatred.

In other words, it's not what you do but why you do it. And you keep coming back to the concept of choice. You seem to be saying something about freedom.

People are choosing all the time, but they don't want to admit it. You are free when you accept the responsibility for your choices.

And when you choose your own best interests. It's not as hard to do as it sounds.

It's hard enough. When I think of all the times I've known I was doing something I'd regret, when it was as clear as day, and I went ahead anyway and ate that extra piece of cake or was irritable toward my mother, I could scream! I can think of hundreds of times I've wanted to be wise and thoughtful and mature and gracious and all those lovely things and ended up acting like a brat.

But that's just what everybody does. Why don't you think about the times you were wise and kind? Why remember and dwell on defeats instead of victories? Many people are under a kind of negative self-hypnosis. They put labels on themselves. They say: I am (a) a terrible person who (b) always does awful things and (c) can't possibly do better. Instead of convincing ourselves beforehand that something we want to do is impossible, we should spend those energies looking for ways to do it. We must encourage ourselves. You can't do anything if you believe you can't. But when you insist you're not the kind of person who can climb a mountain or make a speech, all you are saying is that up to now you haven't done it. Sometimes even that's not true, because if people want to see themselves as unable to do something, they manage to forget the times they actually have done it. But even if they haven't, all they're talking about is their behavior in the past. Who knows what they will do in the future? If we all just kept on doing exactly what we've done up to now, people would never change, and people are changing all the time. That's what growth is: doing things you've never done before, sometimes things you once didn't even dream you could.

*I really never climbed a mountain, and I'm
sure I never will!*

I don't suppose you ever wanted to. Of
course, difficult things are a lot of trouble,
and you have to want to do them very badly.
But when you don't set limits on your efforts,
great things can come out of them.

I remember a young woman, referred to
me by another analyst, who didn't tell me
anything about her at the time. I worked
with her for a year or so, and one day I got a
call from the other analyst. "I ran into Y on
the street the other day," he told me, "and
she looked radiant. She was lively and spar-
kling and happy—what did you do?" I asked
him what was so unusual, and he said, "But
didn't you know, she was a schizophrenic." I
didn't know, and so I hadn't treated her in
terms of a label, and she came along fine. It's
the same with homosexuals. Analysts once
thought they had little chance of changing
homosexuals' preferences and had little success in that direction. But some refused to

accept that and kept working with them, and we've found that a homosexual who really wants to change has a very good chance of doing so. Now we're hearing all kinds of success stories. The nature of homosexuality hasn't changed, but the way of looking at it has.

This is what is meant by a self-fulfilling prophecy. Schoolchildren who are classified as low achievers tend to become low achievers; it has to do with what their teachers expect of them. The children sense that; besides, they always know what type of class they're in, no matter what codes are used. So they learn to expect little of themselves. Many low achievers are simply slow growers or children with problems that interfere with learning but who could do very well, given the right encouragement. It's like what the warden of the Federal House of Detention in Manhattan said recently of his prisoners, "If you treat an individual as he is, he'll stay as he is. But if you treat him as if he were what he ought to be or could be, perhaps he will become that."

We can all do much more than we think, but first we have to believe it. We should try some positive hypnosis for a change.

That sounds like positive thinking, perhaps with a bit of Coué thrown in. "Every day I'm getting better and better": that kind of pep talk is very popular in this country, but I wonder whether it's done more harm than good. Denying difficulties isn't the way to overcome them. It doesn't solve problems; it just helps people avoid facing them. People may have smiles on their faces, but they're dragging the same old anchors around.

It's unfortunate. Positive thinking has more than a grain of truth in it, but it goes too far. Or maybe it doesn't go far enough. When you rely on will power, on "making up your mind," you're using only one of the tools you need to make a change. You do need determination, but good things don't come out of forcing yourself. When you try to do it all out of will power, you are not treating yourself with respect. You are making the assumption that change has to be imposed from above, that your self doesn't have its own impulse to do better. But it does. Real growth can only come from within. You need to learn to work with yourself, to use your will power on the side of yourself. But your self must come willingly. Of course, that doesn't mean you can't use some gentle persuasion.

And your will must be enlisted to help you accomplish what you really *want* to do. Many of us set ourselves arbitrary and impossible goals. Someone who thinks he can do anything he has a "mind" to is not in contact with himself. It is an arrogant belief because it sets no limits. The struggles of our real selves are open-ended, but they are limited by our actual capacities and interests and strivings. It would be futile for me to "make up my mind" to be a painter if I have no talent in that direction. But the truth is, if the talent is lacking, the desire will be absent,

too. Your genuine self does not want to do things that are utterly foreign to it; it wants to realize its own potential. Of course, people can come up with all kinds of crazy notions about what they think they want to do or be, but they are just that—notions, and not genuine impulses. When we use our will power to achieve goals that do not spring out of us, but which we set for the sake of pleasing others or to fulfill a fantasy about who we are, we create a kind of monster, a mechanical man in which our living self is trapped. We have all seen people who are held together by sheer will power; the effort is enormous, but the result is hardly worth it. They aren't people we enjoy being with—or who enjoy being with themselves.

Yet ex-alcoholics often give that impression. You can sense a terrific strain in them; it's costing them a lot. But you can't say the effort

isn't worth it or that it doesn't come from a real desire for liberation.

Yes, that's true. Their tragedy is that many of them don't release their energies from the struggle against what they *don't* want to be, to spend them on becoming the person they *do* want to be. They have taken an important step forward, but they have to go on from there.

What I am trying to say is that if we want to become all that is in us to become, we have to use everything we've got—our feelings, our intuition, our intelligence, and our will power —our whole self. If we do, the payoff is enormous.

Then why don't we do it? Why do so few of us live that way?

Because there's also a hidden payoff in continuing to suffer. For one thing, it's familiar; we're very comfortable with it. It gives us a sense of security to keep on in the same old self-defeating ways, letting one bad action lead to another. We know what to expect. It makes our world comprehensible, predictable, in some sense manageable. One of the things people need most is a feeling of living in a world they understand; that's one of the deepest appeals of religion. That's why people are so disturbed today: it's not only the violence around us, but also the feeling that it doesn't make sense. Nothing seems to hang together any more; the old explanations don't seem to apply.

People don't know what to count on any more. Things seem more and more uncertain.

Social chaos is terrifying, but personal chaos is even more horrifying. From a very early age we are looking for ways to organize that chaos. We all start out as scientists of a sort. Gradually we build an inner view of the world, which sorts out the overwhelming flood of stimuli that come our way, and calls some of them good and desirable and safe and others bad and dangerous. We decide that certain actions will get us the results we want and others are likely to get us into trouble.

How does that come about?

Each of us creates a kind of working hypothesis which says, "This is what life is about." We do that when we're very young, and these theories are often very ingenious

and really help us to survive. The trouble is that too often we don't revise them as we grow older and gain more experience. We keep fitting new experience into the old slots.

I'm sure most people would deny they had any such thing—impressions maybe, some prejudices and associations from things that happened to them as children, but hardly anything as sophisticated as a theory.

Most people don't know they have one, because they have never put it into words. They are made up of vague feelings, unspoken apprehensions, the things we didn't dare talk about or even admit to ourselves as children. They deal with the most powerful and problematic forces in human life, like sex and aggression, which most families find too formidable to discuss. So we develop complex ideas about the nature of reality, which we never communicate and never examine. Someone said that God created the world in a fit of absent-mindedness. We do almost as well. We build worldviews half asleep and let them, like tinted lenses, color our lives.

You mean our most important ideas about life are ones we are not even aware of, and we've been carrying them around since child-hood?

Yes, and their impact can be very powerful. Often when we think we're responding to actual people and events, we're merely assigning them parts in the inner novel we've been writing all our lives. For example, if someone has felt deserted as a child by an

important adult, and this becomes a key experience in his way of seeing the world, there are several ways he can continue to have that experience. One way is to seek out the kind of people who are likely to desert him as an adult—and we are all very clever about that. Another is to drive people away by his own behavior. Or he can imagine he is deserted by people who really haven't mistreated him at all. Whatever way he chooses, he confirms his theory about what to expect from others, and this is very gratifying.

Come on! That certainly doesn't sound like any way to have fun.

You'd be surprised. Being right is one of the most satisfying experiences in the world. Or let's say, rather, that being wrong is one of the most unsettling experiences that can happen to anyone. It's an awful blow to the ego to feel you've made a mistake. That's why people don't want to change. It would mean admitting they were wrong. A patient once burst out at me indignantly, "But that would mean I wasted the first forty years of my life!" Some people would rather go on making the same mistake for another forty years than admit it and cut their losses. People are very stubborn. Sometimes they secretly believe that if they keep on long enough with their misconceived behavior, they'll make it right. That reality will give in to their views, rather than vice versa. They're still trying to get their parents to give in. They haven't given up their anger over what they didn't get when they were five years old.

People feel very justified in that anger; they can give you all the details on how unfairly they were treated. They are usually right; they did get cheated as children. But what they don't see is that they are now cheating themselves as adults. As long as they spend their energies being angry at the

people who deprived them once, they won't spend their effort on getting for themselves what they need now. Their rage isn't hurting their parents, but it's crippling them.

Damn it, it doesn't seem fair. You mean we should just let them get away with it? Wipe the slate clean? After all they put us through?

It isn't fair. Life is not fair. And they did get away with it. There's nothing you can do about that now. There's no way to even the score. Hamlet eventually evened the score, like a lot of other tragic heroes. That can only lead to death, or exile. Electra brought about her mother's death, and never saw her home again. Life lies in another direction. It lies in letting go, in giving up your grievances. You can stop your parents from getting away with

your whole life; you can stop yourself from
giving up your whole life.

*So we just have to write it off? All that suffer-
ing, all those years, all we believed in as children? We have to accept that none of it ever
was what we thought it was?*

But in a sense it was what you thought it
was, then. What people rarely understand is
that they were not wrong at the time they
made up the theories.

*You don't mean that bundle of unspoken ap-
prehensions gave an accurate picture of the
world?*

No, but it was the best way we had of dealing with our corner of the world. We all start out being the smallest, least powerful person in our immediate world, the family. Our helplessness is not a theory; it's a fact. In the early stages of coping with our world, we have to work through others. At five, we need our mother; we must please and pacify her to get the things we need. Our life literally depends on doing so. To accomplish our own thing as children, we must be able to manipulate adults. To get a candy bar or go to the movies, we must win them over. So it is appropriate in childhood to look to others, to learn how to invoke their love, sympathy, and understanding. We can look to ourselves only secondarily. The mistake lies in carrying this sense of helplessness, this need to placate others, into adulthood. What was once a fact has become a fantasy. As an adult, everything doesn't depend on pleasing others. What others once did for you, you can now do for yourself. When you're thirty, you don't need your mother to love you the way she did when you were three. You don't need to feel about her or treat her as you did then.

You don't have to fear her anger any more. You can stop wearing the ties she likes or dating the women she would approve of. That's all over; it's ancient history. You're your own man—or woman—now. But many people will not realize that.

Why not? Why don't they grab that freedom?

They're terribly afraid of losing something they think they cannot do without. You know, the French philosopher Rousseau made a statement that is often quoted: "Man is born free, but everywhere he is in chains." It is closer to the truth to say, "Man is born in chains, but each of us has the potential to be free." Too often people cling to their chains even after they've outgrown them.

Well, yes, I guess it's obvious that people—especially other people—do that. But why in the world do we do it? What are we so afraid to let go of?

It's actually a childlike sense of security we're holding on to. As long as we feel small and helpless, we feel we're in the presence of invisible, all-powerful adults. They may not be very nice adults; we're always expecting them to blame us or yell at us. But as long as they're there, we're not alone. That's the thing we fear most: if that disapproving parent goes away, we will be all by ourselves. But that feeling, too, is a leftover from being four years old. To be abandoned is a terrifying prospect to a child; he literally couldn't survive it. But for an adult, aloneness is something quite different. He not only can survive, he often needs aloneness to grow, to get to know himself and develop his powers. Someone who cannot tolerate aloneness is someone who doesn't know he's grown up.

It takes courage to let go of that fantasy of childhood safety. The world may never seem so certain again, but what fresh air we breathe when we take possession of our own separateness, our own integrity! That's when our adult life really begins.

When you say it, I can feel it. It sounds wonderful and, yet, frightening, too, and somehow bleak. It means being so on your own, so exposed. Something in me pulls back from it. I couldn't say why.

Not only you. Many people hold themselves back from taking that step. The reason is that they have some very distorted ideas about what will happen if they go ahead. It's another childhood myth. When we were small, there was one man and one woman in our world, our parents. They were the big ones, the adults. What a child experiences is, to him, the only way things can be. So he gets

the idea that there can be only one man and one woman, and if anyone has the audacity to set himself up as an adult, he must knock someone else down. He is imbued with a competitive sense of life—to pay Paul you must rob Peter. And this view of life may often be confirmed by his parents, who share the same stingy outlook. If there is not enough to go around, the achievements of one will inevitably be resented by the others. How desperate every action then becomes. If we take our lives into our own hands, it feels like taking life away from someone else. We feel literally as if we are dealing a death blow to our parent. No wonder people hesitate, if the consequences are so devastating. What villains we become if we simply start living our own lives. People can't face feeling like killers, so they back down. But we have to face that feeling, and go ahead anyway. It's the price of self-assertion.

But I don't blame them for backing down. I wouldn't want to feel like a killer. People have enough guilt without that.

You have to live through those feelings if you ever want to grow up completely. What you're killing is not your parents but your fear of them and their power over you. In a very ruthless, primitive way, you have to choose yourself over them. If you go on subordinating your needs and impulses and wishes to theirs, you will never come into your own. If you do make that basic assertion, you will see that no one will end up dead on the battlefield —except old ghosts. Unless, of course, you wait too long, and then reality may accommodate itself to your fantasies. I know someone who imagined that if she ever had a child, it would kill her mother. So she waited until she was forty-five, and, in fact, her mother did die at about the same time. But the outcome is usually much less dramatic.

This economy of emotional scarcity, which is the source of so much jealousy and conflict and resentment, is really a myth. It's a kind

of magical thinking, which vastly exaggerates our impact on the rest of the world. It's not like that at all. What you achieve doesn't take anything away from anyone else. Whatever you do, the world will continue to go about its business. People must compete for real things in the real world, like jobs or scholarships, but that's not what I am talking about. They don't have to compete for their own good opinion. If you become more, it doesn't make me less. There is room for many marvelous people in the world, and many wonderful achievements. When we really grasp this, we take pleasure in what others are able to do; we do not feel diminished. And we are able to do our own thing without feeling anxious or guilty toward anyone.

We actually live in an economy of emotional abundance. There is more than enough to go around. Developing our human resources doesn't use them up; it only enlarges our possibilities. And those resources do not keep. If you do not mine them now, they are lost forever.

That's another thing people don't face. They think they have eternity before them, that what they don't do now, they can do to-morrow or the day after. They think they're playing a game and that if they hold out long enough they'll win. Eventually the other side will give up and give them what they want. But it is not a game; there is no other side. If we hold out long enough, we'll lose all our chances. We don't have eternity; we only have time. It is what we have to work with. There are no limits to how much we can grow and develop, but time limits us. We know this, of course. People are often ob-sessed with aging, with what time does to them. Instead they should be concerned about what they do with time.

It sounds so wise and so beautiful. I would like to wrap it up and take it home with me. But it is so much easier to say it than to do it. Isn't this asking too much of people? Who

*has the power to keep that steady an eye on
reality? I think I know a few things about
life, but I often lose track of them. I get discouraged and impatient and in need of reassurance, and I worry about what might happen in the future. Can people expect to be
that mature?*

They don't have to be totally mature. That's
another thing people don't understand. They
envision adulthood as a door that only opens
out. They think once they step through it they
can never return. Growing up is not a one-
way trip. Adults can be childish, just as children can act very grown up. The two states
aren't mutually exclusive, which is lucky;
otherwise the generations would have more
than a gap. They would face an unbridgeable
abyss. I know that's what many parents think
they face now, but what's usually lacking is
the genuine desire to understand, to make the
imaginative effort, and to accept the fact that
others are different from you.

It's all right to be immature at times; people

who are totally adult are a little intimidating. That's the wonderful thing about marriage. A good marriage is a very adult relationship. But husbands and wives can be all things to each other. You can be parents and playmates, as well as lovers and partners. You can be babied when you need it, and we all do. The only time you run into trouble is when you both want to be babied at the same time, and one of you isn't willing to give it up.

That's very nice to hear, very reassuring. I do feel better knowing I don't have to be a super adult. I think I used to try to do that and it made people feel I was looking down on them; they didn't like it at all.

You didn't feel good about being a child. But there's a child in each of us, and we

should be kind to that child. Another thing people should realize is that when they give up something at twenty-five, they aren't taking it away from their four-year-old self who once had a need for it. Nobody can take away what happened when you were four years old. What you can do is be compassionate to the four-year-old who is still within you. Adults can often be tender toward a four-year-old, but when they find themselves feeling or behaving like one, they react in horror. They become disgusted with themselves, and they disclaim the child they in part still are.

They probably started doing that very early. Somehow in the process of growing up, which should be basically a reaching out to new ways of handling experience, the emphasis shifts to feeling bad about the old ways. This is really the beginning of self-hatred. Genuine growth means having the courage and confidence to try new things, and in the process, to let go of old ones. But you move on because it's more interesting and exciting to take on new challenges; you may be scared, too, but you're also attracted. This doesn't mean you have to despise the self you were. You let go of what you don't need any more because you are on to something better.

That sounds easy, like things just falling into place and appearing when they're needed. But growing isn't easy. It's painful to grow and terribly difficult. You're not sure of where you're going or whether you can get there. There's so much uncertainty, and so much ambivalence.

Of course, of course. Growing pains are very real. And when children are struggling with an important new step forward, they sometimes have to push away their old habits rather violently. They don't need them any more but partly they still do, so their behavior can be quite contrary and unsettling to those around them. Any parent knows what I am talking about. But if that rejection of the

earlier self goes too deep and becomes too
pervasive, the result is not growth, but self-
hatred. The person may learn to do without
satisfying the needs he feels he ought to have
outgrown, but he is impoverished by the effort. We should grow not by turning against
our earlier self but by building on its
strengths. We should recognize that it served
us well, but it's time for something else.

*What is it someone said? That the only way
to true adulthood is through a real childhood.*

Yes. A good childhood is liberating; good
parents help their child move on. The tragedy
of a bad childhood is that people tend to get
hooked on it. They go through life looking
over their shoulder at something they once
had, or thought they had, or wanted. They
waste years trying to recapture the bliss they

had too little of as infants instead of capturing the joy they could have as adults.

~

That's what addicts are often looking for in drugs, isn't it?

Yes. They want to go back for happiness. But it doesn't work. You have to go ahead. It's much harder. Back there you know what to expect—although no one can really get back there, which is why the attempt is so desperate. Going ahead means taking chances, trying things you've never tried. Of all you said earlier—about not being sure of whether you can get there—the hardest thing is when you must give something up and you don't see what you'll get if you do.

That's why people don't want to stop suffering; they know they've got that, and they really don't believe there's anything else. One

of Faulkner's characters said, "Between grief and nothing, I'll take grief." But our choice is between grief and a full life. To take the first steps toward that life may be painful, and you may have to endure sharp pangs of loneliness and loss. But you were lonely anyhow and your loss happened long ago. What you are losing now is only a dream.

It must be a strange awakening. Like opening your eyes for the first time. Like being born.

Only this time you're not so naked. When you are ready to awaken to adulthood, you have what it takes to cope with it.

You said we must take the first steps. What are those steps? How does one start?

The first step is to let go of the dream; rather, to loosen its hold, to begin to give it up, because nobody does it all at once. This is such a basic step that no one can tell anyone how to take it. Something has to dawn. It is partly the dawning of how futile, how unrewarding is the effort to hold on to it. And partly the dawning of a sense that there might be something infinitely more exciting ahead if one does abandon those fruitless efforts.

It makes me think of that old movie, Hold Back the Dawn. *But is there anything people can do to bring on the dawn?*

You start by paying attention. If things

keep turning out the way you don't want them to, ask yourself what you are doing to make them come out that way. See the connection between what you do and how you feel. You may have to sit yourself down and demand some answers. Why do you go on being unkind and unfriendly to yourself? Why do you trip yourself up? What are you getting out of it? What kind of vision of yourself are you holding on to? Do you secretly think that if you act helpless enough, someone will come and take over for you? Do you really think failure will make you lovable?

You talked earlier about the inner novel we've been writing all our lives. This sounds like a form of playacting, going through our part in a private drama, hoping someone will play the other characters we've cast. But if it's all a fantasy, why do we give ourselves such thankless roles?

That's just the point. They're not as thankless as they seem. In all the bad things we do to ourselves, there is usually an expectation of some kind of reward. Punishment, after all, can be a very real reward. Some children feel loved only when they're being punished. The only other thing they get from their parents is indifference, and that's the worst of all. So, as adults, we keep on trying to get a rise out of the people who once mattered to us. We'll put ourselves through all kinds of hell just to feel they're still around. But they're not around any more; we collect no credits for our pains. We've been communing with ghosts—even if they're ghosts of people still alive.

I suppose ghosts can seem better than nothing.

That's the tragedy of it. We think that if we give up the reassurance of those unseen presences, we'll have no one. And it is true that if we let them go, we will have to experience the pain of separation, that sense of aloneness that every mature individual must know. But if you have the courage to endure that wrench and that awareness, it will pave the way for something far better than the childlike dependence you gave up: the true intimacy that is only possible between equals, between adults. That's when the fun really begins. When people are in full possession of themselves, when they really know who they are and *are* who they are, that's when they can really open themselves to others. When you stop trying to get from people what they can't give you, you can begin to enjoy what they can offer. People can share whole worlds with each other, but first they must have access to their own.

You mean for adults intimacy is something quite different from the intimacy a child knows or wants?

And far more enjoyable—for an adult. When the only kind of closeness you can imagine is that of a child to a parent, you may want that closeness desperately, but you have to fear it, too, because in its ultimate form it reduces you, literally, to a gibbering idiot. The last stop in that direction is the womb. If you seek closeness by feeling small and finding protective shelter in someone big, there is always the fear of disappearing altogether. But adult love does not diminish the lover. It enhances us; it makes us more.

You mean the risk of love is not as great as we think.

No one can take the risk out of love; you are offering yourself, and you can always be rejected. When you expose your being to someone, you inevitably take the chance of being hurt. That's why some people prefer not to love at all; they would rather live enclosed in themselves than risk the pain of that exposure, that nakedness that love implies. But an adult, when he loves, does not risk his whole identity. That he already has, and will have however the other responds. If he loses his lover, he will still have himself. But if you look to someone else to establish your identity for you in some way, losing that person can make you really feel destroyed.

You mean that even in the deepest love, you keep a sense of separateness?

At moments of great closeness, there is no

consciousness of separate selves. But that deep sharing of self is different from being swallowed up.

I wouldn't want a life without love in it.

Who would? Everything you do is richer and fuller when love is there. But love is not always there, and how you feel about yourself the times there isn't someone around to receive and return your love has a lot to do with how rewarding the experience of love is when you have it.

I think of a great-aunt of mine, now in her mid-eighties, who lives alone on the edge of the California desert. I once asked her what she did with her time. Her answer was: "There are not enough hours in the day." We visited her recently and found out what she

meant. When we were there, she entertained her literary group, so there was the weekly selection to read in advance and a cake to bake. She also takes a course in creative writing, and between her cultural activities, she raises things in the garden, visits people, and carries on a voluminous correspondence with friends, relatives, and people on radio talk shows. She isn't just making busy-work for herself either; she genuinely enjoys everything she does. A few years ago she took a trip abroad, by herself, and had a wonderful time. She stayed with us awhile on the way back and was a pleasure to have around. She was always glad to spend time with us, but she was perfectly happy when we were busy elsewhere. We never had the feeling she was waiting for us to come and entertain her. She never had that look that says, "Feed me." She had found ways to feed herself.

So we're back to the question of how we go about it. How do we learn to feed ourselves?

It's important to learn to listen to ourselves. Most of us learn to tune ourselves out. We start out receiving our messages loud and clear; babies know when they're hungry and when they hurt. But when we're small, other people's voices are so much louder and surer than our own. It's easiest to go along with what others say. They've got it all figured out already, and we're just starting to put the pieces together. Besides, it's their side the bread is buttered on. If we listen to them, we get room and board. What can we offer ourselves to compete with that? It's another story of what we had to do to survive as children, but we don't need to keep on doing those same things any longer.

Tuning in again takes practice; we have to encourage ourselves to speak up. If we've stopped listening to our own voice for a long time, that voice may be very faint; it may have half given up. It may also be pretty angry for having been shut up so long. But

it's there; we have to give it a chance. If we learn how to listen, we will find out a lot and we will hear some wonderful things.

֍

I suspect we may hear some terrible things, too. Isn't there a lot hidden in us that would be pretty hard to take? That would be too much for people to handle by themselves if it did surface? Isn't that what psychoanalysts are for? To help people dig it up, get it out, sort it out, and maybe, eventually, be free of it?

Analysts can help people a great deal, of course, in delving into the reasons why they mistreat themselves. Some people are so caught up in doing harm to themselves and have so little understanding of why they do it that analysis is the only way they can begin to break out of their self-destructive spiral. It can help them get around the roadblocks that stand in the way of growth—the roadblocks that often were put in place by others but which we work hard to keep there. Analysis is a great tool of liberation. When the first patient lay down on the couch, that was truly a giant step for mankind. But there is so much people can do off the couch. I don't mean to imply that you can't be analyzed sitting up, by the way; I've even done it successfully over the telephone. And there is so much people have to do for themselves, even with an analyst's help. One reason analysis sometimes takes so long is the refusal of many people to realize that, at bottom, change is up to them. No matter how many insights they gain, no matter how much emotional catharsis they may achieve, change does not just happen.

But I have the impression that sometimes change does simply come. I know that has

happened to me. Suddenly you feel very different about someone or something; burdens are lifted; doors open; something you were struggling with becomes easy all at once.

Miracles do seem to happen, and it's a good thing, because they help people keep going. But the struggles must come first. A lot of plugging goes into the making of miracles. They happen to people who are ready for them. But it takes more than these sudden leaps to change a life. It takes a conscious act, a decision to take our life into our hands, and a lot of people don't want to face that decision. They think their analyst is the good father or mother they never had, and that from now on they'll be taken care of. They're partly right, and one of the most important things an analyst can give is his loving interest. But people forget that a good parent is one who helps the child care for himself and take care of himself. Someone has said that if you give a man food, you feed him for a day, but if you teach him how to grow his own, he can feed himself for life.

When you decide to take care of yourself, to take charge of yourself, there is still a big job ahead. It takes thought and effort to shake free of bad habits. A part of you may well be quite indignant at the changes you're trying to make. That part of you that is quite comfortable in the old ways and has no desire to see things or do things differently can put up quite a fight.

A lot of us would rather do almost anything but change. But seriously, it must go much deeper than just changing comfortable habits. There's more at stake than that, surely.

All the things we've been talking about are at stake: our illusions, our fantasies are at stake, our sense of being right about our

world and about ourselves. In a profound sense, a part of one's self feels that its very existence is threatened and is fighting for its survival. It feels like that. But it's a misunderstanding. What is under attack is truly our bad habits, the bad habits of thinking and behaving that have poisoned our lives.

Getting rid of them takes a lot of perseverance. It's not enough to want to change. You must want to want to. You must want to even when you don't want to. There are a lot of ways of putting it. Some of them sound very old-fashioned, like "The price of freedom is eternal vigilance" or "Try and try again." It's corny but true. You have to watch what you're doing. Every time you catch yourself putting yourself down, just stop and turn around and push yourself up.

It takes realism, too. People often want to be perfect and become discouraged when they're not. They have to give that up. Perfection is not for human beings. There may be some perfect works of art, but not so many of those. A perfect person—whatever that would be—would be unbearable. Judging yourself by superhuman standards is another way of mistreating yourself, and a good excuse for giving up. Don't judge yourself at all; accept yourself and move on from there.

Accept the messiness and the mistakes? But I thought the point was to stop making them.

If you do, you'll be the only one.

You know, there's another thing that bothers me, all this watching and working at it all the time. It makes me kind of tired to think about it. It certainly doesn't sound like fun. Where

is that zest we were talking about at the beginning? Where does spontaneity come in?

People often talk about wanting to be spontaneous, to live out of their feelings. They have locked themselves into intellectual boxes, where they hardly know what they feel any more. They become desperate to experience plain, simple emotion. They think if they could throw away their minds, they would be free. That is the appeal of D. H. Lawrence's ideas.

But neither freedom nor feelings are that simple. We have in us a catch-all of programmed reactions—remembered scoldings, schoolbook maxims, nostalgia, and old wives' tales—all mixed up with our own true feelings. So, in practice, "spontaneity" usually means grabbing the first thing that floats to mind and taking it as if it were a message from our depths. But there's a lot of pollution in those depths. We have to examine the reactions that surface to see where the messages really come from. We have to decide which to act on, which represent our true interests. This doesn't mean you have to watch yourself every minute. You don't have to become as self-conscious as the centipede who forgot how to walk. But living out of your own true feelings does take work. If you're willing to invest the effort, the zest will come.

People say they want to "let go." What they really need to do is take hold. Only when you're really in charge of yourself can you afford to let go, to be spontaneous and expect good to come out of it. That's why sex is more satisfying for adults. Only mature people have the self-possession to abandon themselves and know they'll come out of it intact. It sounds like a paradox, but it is one of the secrets of love.

You're convincing me; it sounds better and better. I'm not sure I know enough yet. What else can I do?

You must also learn to talk to yourself. That's very important. You need to explain things, to reassure yourself. You need to establish an on-going dialogue. It can help you through all kinds of tough situations. When the child in you is up to mischief, you can stop and discuss it first; you can tell him "no." There is usually a moment when it could go either way. If you pay attention, you can take that moment and consider what you really want to do. You have the power to stop yourself; this is a good thing to know. At first it's hard, but it gets easier.

It sounds as if man's freedom may hinge on just that little pause. What a narrow margin it is.

You won't always use it well, either. And when the child in you does misbehave, don't punish yourself; you've done that enough. Forgive the child in you. Most of the things you feel terrible about weren't so bad to begin with. We often go on doing things against ourselves just to prove we are the terrible person we imagined we were as a child. We suffer because of such imagined sins as our deep feelings for our parents or our rage when they let us down or our loss of faith in ourselves when another child was born and our star turn was over. We're told to hate the sin and love the sinner, but we're too apt to twist it around the other way. We hate the sinner in us and cling to the sin. Don't glorify your lapses. Just try to understand why they happened and steer yourself back on the right track.

All the kind and thoughtful things you would do toward a living child, all the loving help you would give that child, you can give yourself. When you know a child well, you have a feel for when to put on pressure, when to offer comfort, and when to leave him alone. If you come to know the child in you, you can get that feel for yourself. You can know

when to be easy, when to make demands. You have to get on familiar terms with yourself. Embrace the child in you; make friends with yourself. It gives such a reserve of strength to call on.

I once was seeing a man who was grieving deeply. The person he had been closest to had died, and he felt utterly desolate. I sat with him and could feel the depths of his sorrow. Finally, I said to him, "You look as if you had lost your best friend." He said, "Well, I have." And I said, "Don't you know who your best friend is?" He looked at me, surprised. He thought a moment, and tears came into his eyes. Then he said, "I guess it's true—you are your own best friend."

If we do all of this, if we understand all of these things, will it really make such a difference in our lives?

If we can learn to love and nurture ourselves, we will find our ourselves richer than we ever imagined. We will still be beset by real problems and suffer real defeats. Life is not a picnic—or a rose garden. The world is not run for our benefit. There is no escaping the human condition, which involves pain and difficulty and loss. But we can bring everything we have to bear on the challenges life presents and make the very most of what it offers us. If we liberate ourselves from our fantasies and learn where our real resources lie, a whole world is waiting to be explored.

People often have a need to see themselves as worn out, having tried everything, exhausted their resources, used up everything they have, as if they have given up on themselves. Yet, when we begin to make available to ourselves our own possibilities, it is like drilling a well to an untapped energy reserve, like finding a bank account we haven't yet used. It's the cheapest form of entertainment there is. You never run out; you are never bored. It is also old-age security. When Bernard Berenson, the art critic, was almost ninety, he said, "I would willingly stand at

street corners, hat in hand, begging passers-by to drop their unused minutes into it." He never lost his capacity for enjoying each moment to the full. You can say, "Well, he was an exceptional man." But we can all do it.

It sounds like the secret of living. I wish I could believe we can all learn to live like that.

There is no question that we can. I have seen so many people do it, really come to life. We can all help ourselves to change, to grow, to become the person it is in us to be. We can learn to be our own best friend. If we do, we have a friend for life. We can buoy ourselves up, give ourselves comfort and sustenance the times when there is no one else. We are our best source of encouragement and good advice. We are all accustomed to waiting for someone to give us a kind word, but we really have available to ourselves many kind words.

I feel that I have learned many secrets from you, and heard many wise words. I hope I can remember them.

Of course you'll remember them; you knew them all the time.

About the Authors

Mildred Newman and Bernard Berkowitz are married. Both are practicing psychoanalysts and certified psychologists in New York City, and both are members of the National Psychological Association for Psychoanalysis, the American Psychological Association, and other professional organizations.

Mildred Newman graduated from Hunter College High School and from Hunter College, where she received an M.A. in psychology. Miss Newman spent a number of years in training with the late Theodore Reik, and she completed the analytic training program at

the National Psychological Association for Psychoanalysis. Miss Newman is a supervisor for the Community Guidance Service of New York City, and her work has been anthologized in *New Approaches in Child Guidance* (1970).

Bernard Berkowitz graduated from City College, received an M.S. from Columbia University, and his Ph.D. from New York University. He attended the Alfred Adler Institute and the Postgraduate Center for Mental Health. Dr. Berkowitz has been affiliated with City College and with the John Jay College of Criminal Justice of the City University of New York, and has had numerous articles and reviews published in various journals.

Jean Owen grew up in New Jersey, graduated from Skidmore College, and received an M.A. in philosophy from Columbia University. She had been an audience researcher for a television network, and a writer and editor for an opinion research organization. Miss Owen is married and lives in New York City, where she is a freelance writer.